TEACHER
LESSON PLANNER

♡BELONGS TO:

_____

Teach Love Inspire

Year in Review

August 2022

S	M	T	W	T	F	S
	1	2	3	4	5	6
7	8	9	10	11	12	13
14	15	16	17	18	19	20
21	22	23	24	25	26	27
28	29	30	31			

September 2022

S	M	T	W	T	F	S
				1	2	3
4	5	6	7	8	9	10
11	12	13	14	15	16	17
18	19	20	21	22	23	24
25	26	27	28	29	30	

October 2022

S	M	T	W	T	F	S
						1
2	3	4	5	6	7	8
9	10	11	12	13	14	15
16	17	18	19	20	21	22
23	24	25	26	27	28	29
30	31					

November 2022

S	M	T	W	T	F	S
		1	2	3	4	5
6	7	8	9	10	11	12
13	14	15	16	17	18	19
20	21	22	23	24	25	26
27	28	29	30			

December 2022

S	M	T	W	T	F	S
				1	2	3
4	5	6	7	8	9	10
11	12	13	14	15	16	17
18	19	20	21	22	23	24
25	26	27	28	29	30	31

January 2023

S	M	T	W	T	F	S
1	2	3	4	5	6	7
8	9	10	11	12	13	14
15	16	17	18	19	20	21
22	23	24	25	26	27	28
29	30	31				

February 2023

S	M	T	W	T	F	S
		1	2	3	4	
5	6	7	8	9	10	11
12	13	14	15	16	17	18
19	20	21	22	23	24	25
26	27	28				

March 2023

S	M	T	W	T	F	S
			1	2	3	4
5	6	7	8	9	10	11
12	13	14	15	16	17	18
19	20	21	22	23	24	25
26	27	28	29	30	31	

April 2023

S	M	T	W	T	F	S
						1
2	3	4	5	6	7	8
9	10	11	12	13	14	15
16	17	18	19	20	21	22
23	24	25	26	27	28	29
30						

May 2023

S	M	T	W	T	F	S
	1	2	3	4	5	6
7	8	9	10	11	12	13
14	15	16	17	18	19	20
21	22	23	24	25	26	27
28	29	30	31			

June 2023

S	M	T	W	T	F	S
				1	2	3
4	5	6	7	8	9	10
11	12	13	14	15	16	17
18	19	20	21	22	23	24
25	26	27	28	29	30	

July 2023

S	M	T	W	T	F	S
						1
2	3	4	5	6	7	8
9	10	11	12	13	14	15
16	17	18	19	20	21	22
23	24	25	26	27	28	29
30	31					

Holidays list

2022	2023	OBSERVANCES	NOTES
Jan 1	Jan 1	New Year's Day	
Jan 17	Jan 16	Martin Luther King Jr. Day	
Feb 14	Feb 14	Valentine's Day	
Feb 21	Feb 20	Presidents' Day (US)	
Mar 13	Mar 12	Daylight Saving Time begins (US / CAN)	
Mar 17	Mar 17	St. Patrick's Day	
Mar 27	Mar 19	Mother's Day (UK) *	
Mar 27	Mar 26	Daylight Saving Time begins (UK) *	
Apr 17	Apr 9	Easter Sunday	
Apr 18	Apr 18	Tax Day (US)	
May 2	May 1	May Day (UK)*	
May 5	May 5	Cinco de Mayo	
May 14	May 14	Mother's Day (US / CAN)	
May 29	May 29	Memorial Day (US)	
May 30	May 29	Victoria Day (CAN)	
Jun 1	May 29	Spring Bank Holiday (UK) *	
Jun 14	Jun 14	Flag Day (US)	
Jun 18	Jun 18	Father's Day	
Jun 19	Jun 19	Juneteenth	
Jul 1	Jul 1	Canada Day	
Jul 4	Jul 4	Independence Day (US)	
Aug 29	Aug 28	August Bank Holiday (UK)*	
Sep 5	Sep 5	Labor/Labour Day (US / CAN)	
Sep 11	Sep 11	Patriot Day (US)	
Oct 10	Oct 10	Columbus Day (US)	
Oct 10	Oct 9	Thanksgiving (CAN)	
Oct 29	Oct 29	Daylight Saving Time Ends (UK)*	
Oct 31	Oct 31	Halloween	
Nov 6	Nov 5	Daylight Saving Time Ends (US / CAN)	
Nov 7	Nov 7	Election Day (US)	
Nov 11	Nov 11	Veterans Day (US)	
Nov 11	Nov 11	Remembrance Day (CAN)	
Nov 23	Nov 23	Thanksgiving Day (US)	
Nov 24	Nov 24	Black Friday	
Dec 24	Dec 24	Christmas Eve	
Dec 25	Dec 25	Christmas Day	
Dec 31	Dec 31	New Year's Eve	

Important dates

AUGUST
- _____
- _____
- _____
- _____
- _____

SEPTEMBER
- _____
- _____
- _____
- _____
- _____

OCTOBER
- _____
- _____
- _____
- _____
- _____

NOVEMBER
- _____
- _____
- _____
- _____
- _____

DECEMBER
- _____
- _____
- _____
- _____
- _____

JANUARY
- _____
- _____
- _____
- _____
- _____

FEBRUARY
- _____
- _____
- _____
- _____
- _____

MARCH
- _____
- _____
- _____
- _____
- _____

APRIL
- _____
- _____
- _____
- _____
- _____

MAY
- _____
- _____
- _____
- _____
- _____

JUNE
- _____
- _____
- _____
- _____
- _____

JULY
- _____
- _____
- _____
- _____
- _____

Birthdays

AUGUST

- ◆ _____
- ◆ _____
- ◆ _____
- ◆ _____
- ◆ _____

SEPTEMBER

- ◆ _____
- ◆ _____
- ◆ _____
- ◆ _____
- ◆ _____

OCTOBER

- ◆ _____
- ◆ _____
- ◆ _____
- ◆ _____
- ◆ _____

NOVEMBER

- ◆ _____
- ◆ _____
- ◆ _____
- ◆ _____
- ◆ _____

DECEMBER

- ◆ _____
- ◆ _____
- ◆ _____
- ◆ _____
- ◆ _____

JANUARY

- ◆ _____
- ◆ _____
- ◆ _____
- ◆ _____
- ◆ _____

FEBRUARY

- ◆ _____
- ◆ _____
- ◆ _____
- ◆ _____
- ◆ _____

MARCH

- ◆ _____
- ◆ _____
- ◆ _____
- ◆ _____
- ◆ _____

APRIL

- ◆ _____
- ◆ _____
- ◆ _____
- ◆ _____
- ◆ _____

MAY

- ◆ _____
- ◆ _____
- ◆ _____
- ◆ _____
- ◆ _____

JUNE

- ◆ _____
- ◆ _____
- ◆ _____
- ◆ _____
- ◆ _____

JULY

- ◆ _____
- ◆ _____
- ◆ _____
- ◆ _____
- ◆ _____

Class list

FIRST NAME	LAST NAME	CONTACT	PARENTS	COMMENTS

Timetable

	MONDAY	TUESDAY	WEDNESDAY	THURSDAY	FRIDAY

Seating Chart

Attendance record

Grade record

monthly & weekly
LESSON PLANNER

August 2022

SUNDAY	MONDAY	TUESDAY	WEDNESDAY
	1	2	3
7	8	9	10
14	15	16	17
21	22	23	24
28	29	30	31

favorite Quote:

THURSDAY	FRIDAY	SATURDAY
4	5	6
11	12	13
18	19	20
25	26	27

To do list:

◆ _____
◆ _____
◆ _____
◆ _____
◆ _____
◆ _____
◆ _____
◆ _____
◆ _____

Notes

_____
_____
_____
_____
_____
_____
_____
_____
_____
_____
_____

1 august - 7 august 2022

Subject	Monday [1]	Tuesday [2]	Wednesday [3]

Thursday 4	Friday 5

Saturday 6

Sunday 7

Notes

8 august - 14 august 2022

Subject	Monday	8	Tuesday	9	Wednesday	10

Thursday	11	Friday	12

Saturday	13

Sunday	14

Notes

15 august - 21 august 2022

Subject	Monday	15	Tuesday	16	Wednesday	17

Thursday	18	Friday	19

Saturday	20

Sunday	21

Notes

22 august - 28 august 2022

Subject	Monday	22	Tuesday	23	Wednesday	24

Thursday 25	Friday 26

Saturday 27

Sunday 28

Notes

September 2022

SUNDAY	MONDAY	TUESDAY	WEDNESDAY
4	5	6	7
11	12	13	14
18	19	20	21
25	26	27	28

favorite Quote.

THURSDAY	FRIDAY	SATURDAY
1	2	3
8	9	10
15	16	17
22	23	24
29	30 *first day of autumn*	

To do list:

◆ _____
◆ _____
◆ _____
◆ _____
◆ _____
◆ _____
◆ _____
◆ _____
◆ _____

Notes

_____
_____
_____
_____
_____
_____
_____
_____
_____

29 august - 4 september 2022

Subject	Monday	29	Tuesday	30	Wednesday	31

Thursday 1	Friday 2

Saturday 3

Sunday 4

Notes

5 september - 11 september 2022

Subject	Monday	5	Tuesday	6	Wednesday	7

Thursday	8	Friday	9

Saturday	10

Sunday	11

Notes

12 september - 18 september 2022

Subject	Monday	12	Tuesday	13	Wednesday	14

Thursday	15	Friday	16

Saturday	17

Sunday	18

Notes

19 september - 25 september 2022

Subject	Monday	19	Tuesday	20	Wednesday	21

Thursday	22	Friday	23

Saturday	24

Sunday	25

Notes

October 2022

SUNDAY	MONDAY	TUESDAY	WEDNESDAY
2	3	4	5
9	10	11	12
16	17	18	19
23	24	25	26
30	31		

THURSDAY	FRIDAY	SATURDAY
		1
6	7	8
13	14	15
20	21	22
27	28	29

To do list:

◆ _____
◆ _____
◆ _____
◆ _____
◆ _____
◆ _____
◆ _____
◆ _____
◆ _____

Notes

_____
_____
_____
_____
_____
_____
_____
_____
_____
_____

26 september - 2 october 2022

Subject	Monday	26	Tuesday	27	Wednesday	28

Thursday 29	Friday 30

Saturday 1

Sunday 2

Notes

3 october – 9 october 2022

Subject	Monday 3	Tuesday 4	Wedresday 5

Thursday	6	Friday	7

Saturday	8

Sunday	9

Notes

10 october - 16 october 2022

Subject	Monday	10	Tuesday	11	Wednesday	12

Thursday	13	Friday	14

Saturday	15

Sunday	16

Notes

17 october - 23 october 2022

Subject	Monday	17	Tuesday	18	Wednesday	19

Thursday 20	Friday 21

Saturday 22

Sunday 23

Notes

24 october - 30 october 2022

Subject	Monday 24	Tuesday 25	Wednesday 26

Thursday 27	Friday 28

Saturday 29

Sunday 30

Notes

November 2022

SUNDAY	MONDAY	TUESDAY	WEDNESDAY
		1	2
6	7	8	9
13	14	15	16
20	21	22	23
27	28	29	30

favorite Quote.

THURSDAY	FRIDAY	SATURDAY
3	4	5
10	11	12
17	18	19
24	25	26

To do list:

◆ _____
◆ _____
◆ _____
◆ _____
◆ _____
◆ _____
◆ _____
◆ _____
◆ _____

Notes

_____
_____
_____
_____
_____
_____
_____
_____
_____
_____

31 october - 6 november 2022

Subject	Monday 31	Tuesday 1	Wednesday 2

Thursday	3	Friday	4

Saturday	5

Sunday	6

Notes

7 november - 13 november 2022

Subject	Monday 7	Tuesday 8	Wednesday 9

Thursday	10	Friday	11

Saturday	12

Sunday	13

Notes

14 november - 20 november 2022

Subject	Monday	14	Tuesday	15	Wednesday	16

Thursday	17	Friday	18

Saturday	19

Sunday	20

Notes

21 november - 27 november 2022

Subject	Monday 21	Tuesday 22	Wednesday 23

Thursday	24	Friday	25

Saturday	26

Sunday	27

Notes

December 2022

SUNDAY	MONDAY	TUESDAY	WEDNESDAY
4	5	6	7
11	12	13	14
18	19	20	21 *first day of winter*
25	26	27	28

favorite Quote.

THURSDAY	FRIDAY	SATURDAY
1	2	3
8	9	10
15	16	17
22	23	24
29	30	31

To do list:

◆ _____
◆ _____
◆ _____
◆ _____
◆ _____
◆ _____
◆ _____
◆ _____
◆ _____

Notes

_____
_____
_____
_____
_____
_____
_____
_____
_____
_____

28 november - 4 december 2022

Subject	Monday	28	Tuesday	29	Wednesday	30

Week:

Thursday 1	Friday 2

Saturday 3

Sunday 4

Notes

5 december - 11 december 2022

Subject	Monday	5	Tuesday	6	Wednesday	7

Thursday 8	Friday 9

Saturday 10

Sunday 11

Notes

12 december - 18 december 2022

Subject	Monday	12	Tuesday	13	Wednesday	14

Thursday 15	Friday 16

Saturday 17

Sunday 18

Notes

19 december - 25 december 2022

Subject	Monday	19	Tuesday	20	Wednesday	21

Thursday	22	Friday	23

Saturday	24

Sunday	25

Notes

January 2023

SUNDAY	MONDAY	TUESDAY	WEDNESDAY
1	2	3	4
8	9	10	11
15	16	17	18
22	23	24	25
29	30	31	

 *favorite Quote.*

THURSDAY	FRIDAY	SATURDAY
5	6	7
12	13	14
19	20	21
26	27	28

To do list:

◆ _____

◆ _____

◆ _____

◆ _____

◆ _____

◆ _____

◆ _____

◆ _____

◆ _____

Notes

_____

_____

_____

_____

_____

_____

_____

_____

_____

_____

26 december 2022 - 1 january 2023

Subject	Monday	26	Tuesday	27	Wednesday	28

Thursday 29	Friday 30

Saturday 31

Sunday 1

Notes

2 january - 8 january 2023

Subject	Monday	2	Tuesday	3	Wednesday	4

Thursday	5	Friday	6

Saturday	7

Sunday	8

Notes

9 january - 15 january 2023

Subject	Monday	9	Tuesday	10	Wednesday	11

Thursday	12	Friday	13

Saturday	14

Sunday	15

Notes

16 january – 22 january 2023

Subject	Monday 16	Tuesday 17	Wednesday 18

Thursday 19	Friday 20

Saturday 21

Sunday 22

Notes

23 january - 29 january 2023

Subject	Monday	23	Tuesday	24	Wednesday	25

Thursday	26	Friday	27

Saturday	28

Sunday	29

Notes

february 2023

SUNDAY	MONDAY	TUESDAY	WEDNESDAY
			1
5	6	7	8
12	13	14	15
19	20	21	22
26	27	28	

THURSDAY	FRIDAY	SATURDAY
2	3	4
9	10	11
16	17	18
23	24	25

To do list:

◆ _____

◆ _____

◆ _____

◆ _____

◆ _____

◆ _____

◆ _____

◆ _____

◆ _____

Notes

_____

_____

_____

_____

_____

_____

_____

_____

_____

_____

_____

30 january - 5 february 2023

Subject	Monday 30	Tuesday 31	Wednesday 1

Thursday 2	Friday 3

Saturday 4

Sunday 5

Notes

6 february – 12 february 2023

Subject	Monday	6	Tuesday	7	Wednesday	8

Thursday 9	Friday 10

Saturday 11

Sunday 12

Notes

13 february - 19 february 2023

Subject	Monday 13	Tuesday 14	Wednesday 15

Week: ....

Thursday 16	Friday 17

Saturday 18

Sunday 19

Notes

20 february - 26 february 2023

Subject	Monday 20	Tuesday 21	Wednesday 22

Thursday	23	Friday	24

Saturday	25

Sunday	26

Notes

March 2023

SUNDAY	MONDAY	TUESDAY	WEDNESDAY
			1
5	6	7	8
12	13	14	15
19	20 *first day of spring*	21	22
26	27	28	29

THURSDAY	FRIDAY	SATURDAY
2	3	4
9	10	11
16	17	18
23	24	25
30	31	

To do list:

◆ _____
◆ _____
◆ _____
◆ _____
◆ _____
◆ _____
◆ _____
◆ _____
◆ _____

Notes

_____
_____
_____
_____
_____
_____
_____
_____
_____
_____

27 february - 5 march 2023

Subject	Monday	27	Tuesday	28	Wednesday	1

Thursday	2	Friday	3

Saturday	4

Sunday	5

Notes

6 march - 12 march 2023

Subject	Monday	6	Tuesday	7	Wednesday	8

Week:

Thursday 9	Friday 10

Saturday 11

Sunday 12

Notes

13 march - 19 march 2023

Subject	Monday	13	Tuesday	14	Wednesday	15

Thursday	16	Friday	17

Saturday	18

Sunday	19

Notes

20 march - 26 march 2023

Subject	Monday 20	Tuesday 21	Wednesday 22

Thursday 23	Friday 24

Saturday 25

Sunday 26

Notes

April 2023

SUNDAY	MONDAY	TUESDAY	WEDNESDAY
2	3	4	5
9	10	11	12
16	17	18	19
23	24	25	26
30			

 favorite Quote.

THURSDAY	FRIDAY	SATURDAY
		1
6	7	8
13	14	15
20	21	22
27	28	29

To do list:

◆ _____
◆ _____
◆ _____
◆ _____
◆ _____
◆ _____
◆ _____
◆ _____
◆ _____

Notes

_____
_____
_____
_____
_____
_____
_____
_____
_____

27 march - 2 april 2023

Subject	Monday	27	Tuesday	28	Wednesday	29

Thursday 30	Friday 31

Saturday 1

Sunday 2

Notes

3 april – 9 april 2023

Subject	Monday 3	Tuesday 4	Wednesday 5

Thursday	6	Friday	7

Saturday	8

Sunday	9

Notes

10 april - 16 april 2023

Subject	Monday 10	Tuesday 11	Wednesday 12

Thursday 13	Friday 14

Saturday 15

Sunday 16

Notes

17 april - 23 april 2023

Subject	Monday 17	Tuesday 18	Wednesday 19

Week:

Thursday 20	Friday 21

Saturday 22

Sunday 23

Notes

24 april - 30 april 2023

Subject	Monday	24	Tuesday	25	Wednesday	26

Thursday 27	Friday 28

Saturday 29

Sunday 30

Notes

May 2023

SUNDAY	MONDAY	TUESDAY	WEDNESDAY
	1	2	3
7	8	9	10
14	15	16	17
21	22	23	24
28	29	30	31

favorite Quote.

THURSDAY	FRIDAY	SATURDAY
4	5	6
11	12	13
18	19	20
25	26	27

To do list:

◆ _____
◆ _____
◆ _____
◆ _____
◆ _____
◆ _____
◆ _____
◆ _____
◆ _____

Notes

_____
_____
_____
_____
_____
_____
_____
_____
_____
_____

1 may – 7 may 2023

Subject	Monday 1	Tuesday 2	Wednesday 3

Thursday 4	Friday 5

Saturday 6

Sunday 7

Notes

8 may - 14 may 2023

Subject	Monday	8	Tuesday	9	Wednesday	10

Thursday	11	Friday	12

Saturday	13

Sunday	14

Notes

15 may - 21 may 2023

Subject	Monday	15	Tuesday	16	Wednesday	17

Thursday	18	Friday	19

Saturday	20

Sunday	21

Notes

22 may - 28 may 2023

Subject	Monday	22	Tuesday	23	Wednesday	24

Thursday	25	Friday	26

Saturday	27

Sunday	28

Notes

June 2023

SUNDAY	MONDAY	TUESDAY	WEDNESDAY
4	5	6	7
11	12	13	14
18	19	20	21 *first day of summer*
25	26	27	28

favorite Quote:

THURSDAY	FRIDAY	SATURDAY
1	2	3
8	9	10
15	16	17
22	23	24
29	30	

To do list:

◆ _____
◆ _____
◆ _____
◆ _____
◆ _____
◆ _____
◆ _____
◆ _____
◆ _____

Notes

_____
_____
_____
_____
_____
_____
_____
_____
_____

29 may - 4 june 2023

Subject	Monday 29	Tuesday 30	Wednesday 31

Thursday	1	Friday	2

Saturday	3

Sunday	4

Notes

5 june - 11 june 2023

Subject	Monday	5	Tuesday	6	Wednesday	7

Thursday	8	Friday	9

Saturday	10

Sunday	11

Notes

12 june - 18 june 2023

Subject	Monday	12	Tuesday	13	Wednesday	14

Thursday	15	Friday	16

Saturday	17

Sunday	18

Notes

19 june - 25 june 2023

Subject	Monday 19	Tuesday 20	Wednesday 21

Thursday 22	Friday 23

Saturday 24

Sunday 25

Notes

July 2023

SUNDAY	MONDAY	TUESDAY	WEDNESDAY
2	3	4	5
9	10	11	12
16	17	18	19
23	24	25	26
30	31		

favorite Quote.

THURSDAY	FRIDAY	SATURDAY
		1
6	7	8
13	14	15
20	21	22
27	28	29

To do list:

◆ _____
◆ _____
◆ _____
◆ _____
◆ _____
◆ _____
◆ _____
◆ _____
◆ _____

Notes

_____
_____
_____
_____
_____
_____
_____
_____
_____
_____

26 june - 2 july 2023

Subject	Monday	26	Tuesday	27	Wednesday	28

Thursday 29	Friday 30

Saturday 1

Sunday 2

Notes

3 july - 9 july 2023

Subject	Monday	3	Tuesday	4	Wednesday	5

Thursday	6	Friday	7

Saturday	8

Sunday	9

Notes

10 july - 16 july 2023

Subject	Monday	10	Tuesday	11	Wednesday	12

Thursday	13	Friday	14

Saturday	15

Sunday	16

Notes

17 july - 23 july 2023

Subject	Monday 17	Tuesday 18	Wednesday 19

Thursday	20	Friday	21

Saturday	22

Sunday	23

Notes

24 july - 30 july 2023

Subject	Monday 24	Tuesday 25	Wednesday 26

Thursday	27	Friday	28

Saturday	29

Sunday	30

Notes

31 july - 6 august 2023

Subject	Monday 31	Tuesday 1	Wednesday 2

Thursday 3	Friday 4

Saturday 5

Sunday 6

Notes

Thank You!

2022-2023 Teacher Planner

so much for trying our Teacher Planner!

We'd love to hear from you!

If you've found this to be a good book please,

support us and leave a review.

If you have any suggestions or issues with this book, or if

you want to test some of our latest notebooks

please email us.

Send email to:

pickme.readme@gmail.com